Be Your Own Equalizer

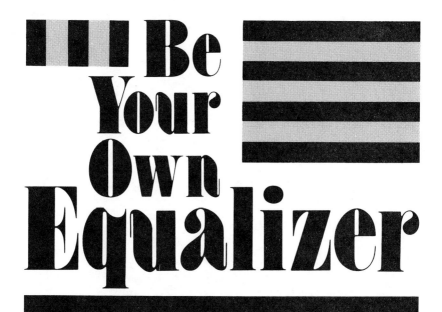

Be Your Own Equalizer

How to Fight the System and Win

Victor Santoro

PALADIN PRESS
BOULDER, COLORADO

Be Your Own Equalizer:
How to Fight the System and Win
by Victor Santoro

Copyright © 1990 by Victor Santoro

ISBN 0-87364-551-0
Printed in the United States of America

Published by Paladin Press, a division of
Paladin Enterprises, Inc., P.O. Box 1307,
Boulder, Colorado 80306, USA.
(303) 443-7250

Direct inquiries and/or orders to the above address.

Visit our Web site at www.paladin-press.com

CONTENTS

INTRODUCTION

From the moment we're born, most of us face an unequal struggle. We're exploited by people who are more powerful, better organized, and often smarter than ourselves. They spend a good deal of their time and effort to see that they remain that way. Despite the propaganda about all men being created equal, we're not; and the people in power have a vested interest in seeing that the people below them remain there. To ensure this, they have created a system to keep these unfortunate people at a disadvantage.

You can't beat the system by open defiance. It is true that you can't fight city hall. If you stand up and defy it, you'll get your head knocked off. Where does this leave the little guy, the inoffensive middle-of-the-road person who just wants to get along in life but faces an unequal contest?

Survival in the real world is not a matter of being prepared for nuclear war, invasion, or civil uprising. It's a matter of coping with the day-to-day stressors and the long-term exploitation by the people in power. It's defending yourself against people and institutions, such as

1

the post office, that are supposed to serve you but actually serve only themselves.

Each of us can conduct his own guerrilla war against the system. It requires brains, not brawn. It's nonviolent and nonconfrontational. It's a matter of survival, not revenge, because the purpose is to avoid being victimized, not to right a wrong after it's been committed. Avoiding problems is far less stressful than coping with them after they happen and trying to decide if it's worth the trouble to get the person or institution that wronged you.

It boils down to adopting a street-smart attitude and concentrating on working the angles instead of beating your head against a wall. By concentrating on defenses against any unethical tactics you're likely to encounter, this book will show you ways to avoid being victimized and to turn situations around to exploit the victimizers.

Avoidance is better than conflict in many cases. You can't fight the big boys because they're more powerful than you are. You also can't fight them on their home ground or by their rules. That's a sure prescription for losing. Instead, you have to avoid certain losing situations that are designed to leave you with no escape and no recourse. In this book, we'll discuss avoidance as well as countermeasures.

This book wasn't written as a consumer-report alert about shoddy marketing practices and products. That information is available elsewhere. This book also is not intended to teach you how to find a job or write a résumé. Those nineteenth-century tactics don't work against twentieth-century technology. But this book *will* show you how to cope in the real world, against the people and institutions that try to take unfair advantage of you. *Be Your Own Equalizer* is a survival manual for the nineties.

ATTITUDE

First, you have to abandon the conventional notions of right and wrong. Those in control of our social, political, economic, and educational institutions program these values into you at an early age so you'll be a docile employee and consumer. The people in power want you to obey a code of conduct that they, in turn, violate daily.

This is why schools stress certain forms of behavior, such as honesty and promptness, which will be valuable to an employer. They also stress the myth that security comes from a steady job, and that an employee should be grateful to his employer for giving him a job. Modern American education is business-oriented, aimed at turning out a corps of obedient employees and consumers. Educators don't teach defense tactics against exploitation, such as how to shop for price and quality, or how to get the most out of your relationship with your employer.

To learn to defend yourself against the system, you first have to deprogram yourself from these indoctrinated attitudes. You must realize that it's futile to work according to a set of rules that those in power establish yet regularly

3

violate. They have set the rules to keep you in place, while they exploit the system for all they can get.

Newspaper headlines show that the rich and powerful people in this country are just as immoral as the members of what we call organized crime. In fact, they form a part of the organized-crime network. It's just that this segment of organized crime has more equal-opportunity enrollment practices. They don't require their members to belong to a particular ethnic or religious group; merely, that they uphold the unwritten code of keeping the rich on top and the poor underfoot. For instance, insider-trading secrets and defense-contract irregularities provide some of this country's biggest criminals with an easy living. They live the high life while the rest of us sweat out a marginal existence. This is why you have to reorient your thinking.

Learn to look at life from the traditional blue-collar viewpoint. Don't accept the counterfeit idea that all Americans are middle class. Unless you were born wealthy, you're probably working class. To defend yourself properly, you have to adopt street-smart attitudes and techniques to replace what has been programmed into you.

An important point of the blue-collar ethic is that it's only wrong to steal from another working-class person. It's okay to steal from the rich; they can afford the loss and probably got their money by stealing from others anyway. Blue-collar ethics condone stealing from the boss, but not from fellow employees. Large, wealthy institutions, such as banks and governmental agencies, make natural targets for a little creative redistribution. Banks hold your money, but according to their rules, and often they will disclose your financial affairs to the Internal Revenue Service (IRS) without your consent. Government officials take your money without your consent, through taxation, and then waste most of it.

Another important point is to be realistic. Don't waste your time dreaming of winning the state lottery or committing the perfect crime that will net you a million dollars. Even if you could get into the vault of the First National Bank and make off with a million, you can be certain that the theft will be noticed immediately, and your chances of getting away are slim.

Instead, think small. Bigger is not necessarily better. Get what's yours bit by bit and avoid making waves. Develop your patience and be satisfied with victory on the installment plan. It's safer to keep a low profile, as we'll see as we study the subject further.

Another lesson to learn quickly is when and how to choose a helper. Some techniques outlined in this book require assistance. It's best to work with someone who has as much to gain and lose as you do. This ensures loyalty on both sides.

Let's begin by looking at a few ways to defend yourself against income taxes, which the government uses to rape you economically.

INCOME TAXES

Despite the rhetoric and Reagan's 1986 Tax Reform Act, the U.S. tax code still gives big breaks to the rich and taps working people for the bulk of the government's income. Careful planning is required so you don't give away more than you absolutely have to.

Although the rules regarding how much you're allowed in interest and other deductions have changed, the same basic fact remains: you should have paperwork to document every deduction you claim. The only exception to this is religious contributions. If you go to church, claim more contributions than you actually give. If you don't go to church, claim them anyway. IRS agents don't check these because it's impossible to determine who actually goes to church and who contributes how much.

Interest

The IRS requires you to document interest deductions. Following the principle that paperwork is the magic key to supporting deductions, take out a loan for the next major purchase that is in a category you can deduct. Then, pay the loan off early, and use the original contract to support your interest deduction. Few IRS agents will have the persistence to ask to see every check.

Receipts

Running your own business gives you a virtual license to steal, if you save all of the receipts. A receipt from a department store that does not list the item purchased provides a piece of paper you can claim. You simply list it as a purchase relevant to your business.

If push comes to shove, create your own receipts. You can't, however, just type up phony bills. They have to look realistic enough to support a few deductions. To do this effectively, you must be prepared.

Start collecting letterheads and business cards everywhere you go. If you go to a motel, take a few pieces of their letterhead. Ask for a business card at each company you visit or from each business representative you meet. These can serve as improvised receipts, allowing you to double your deductible expenses. While on business trips, write extra receipts. If the IRS audits you, simply show them this paperwork to support your deductions. If an auditor asks why a certain receipt is written rather than printed, simply say that the computer was broken that day, so the clerk wrote your bill.

Creating bills from scratch is just as easy. Whenever you're in a stationery store, keep an eye out for receipt books and pads. Since each usually costs less than a dollar, buy some in different sizes, colors, and paper stock. With these, you can generate extra receipts that will pass scrutiny.

Note the critical word in the last paragraph: few. Think small. Don't get greedy. If you list so many deductions that it makes it impossible to live on your earnings, the IRS will become suspicious. Lastly, forget about any tax-shelter schemes. They're designed to provide a nice living for sharp-talking salesman, not to help you to avoid the IRS. You work hard to earn your money, so you want to keep as much as you can.

For most people, earning money means finding a job, and one hazard they often encounter in these rough waters is the killer shark known as an employment agency.

DEALING WITH EMPLOYMENT AGENCIES

Did you ever notice that private employment agencies seem to have a corner on all the good jobs? Does it seem that state employment offices offer only menial and minimum-wage jobs? You may not be aware of another problem with state employment services. Affirmative-action laws require that they give preference to minority group members. If you are not a minority member, but still need a job, you'll get second pickings.

Of course, state agencies list government jobs, but there's a catch. For these, you have to fill out a job application and wait for months before the next testing period comes up. If you pass the test, your name goes on a list (with all the others who have passed) to wait for a job opening. That's not much help if you need a job right now. Your choice, then, is limited to minimum-wage jobs, such as frying hamburgers or pumping gasoline.

Why do private employment agencies have so many attractive jobs to offer? If you look at the contract you have to sign when you seek their services, you'll see that for each job they fill, they receive a fee, usually paid by the jobholder. This fee often amounts to hundreds or thousands of dollars, depending on what the job pays. Laws regulating fees vary from state to state, but most have a minimum fee and a percentage-based sliding scale. For a relatively low-paying job, the jobhunter will have to pay, for example, one month's salary. If the yearly salary is more than a certain amount, the agencies charge a percentage of the earnings, which can easily amount to several months' pay. (As a concession to reality, clients are allowed to pay this fee in monthly installments.)

Let's see why this screws you, the jobseeker. The function of an employment agency is to find qualified people for the employer to hire. In short, the agency is working for him. However, you're paying the fee. Is that fair? Of course not, but private employment agencies have operated this way for decades. By contrast, state employment services find jobs for jobseekers and there is no fee involved. Since some private agencies offer kickbacks to personnel managers to get their job openings, some employers don't bother listing their jobs with state agencies.

Encouraging to jobhunters, however, is the increase in the number of employment ads run by private agencies stressing that the employer will pay all fees. If you can land such a job, grab it. If you have to pay the fee, you'll find it painful. Between withholding taxes and the installments on the employment-agency fees, you'll find your budget painfully tight for several months.

Agency fees are hard to avoid. Standard practice calls for the applicant to sign a contract when he fills out the application form. The agent won't even speak to an applicant until the paperwork is completed and the contract signed. A receptionist usually handles the paperwork in the outer office to prevent prospective clients from picking up any job leads from papers on the agents' desks.

You can get a job through an agency and not pay, however, by not signing the contract yourself. Instead, team up with a friend or acquaintance who's also looking for a job, and apply for each other's job prospects. He shows up at the employment agency advertising the job you want, signs the form, and gets the referral slips with the companies' names and addresses. You do the same for him. Then you exchange referral slips, copy the addresses, throw the slips away, and go after the jobs you want. When you interview for a job, don't mention the employment agency. Instead, explain you are canvassing companies in your line of business. This will get you in most of the time, except with the companies in which the personnel manager is getting a kickback and won't consider anyone not referred by the employment agency.

If you get the job, there's nothing the employment agency can do, because they don't have your signature on any contract. In fact, they've never seen or heard of you. The person who signed their contract never applied for the job. You're home free!

Other Choices

Jobhunters can explore the market in other ways. Some companies advertise directly or through blind ads in newspapers and trade journals. Blind ads don't list the company—usually just a post-office box—for any of several reasons. The employer may be seeking to replace someone without being inundated with telephone calls and personal visits. He also may be exploring the job market to determine the size of the labor pool. Or he may be somewhat paranoid and is running his version of a loyalty test, in which case any of his employees who answer will have a hard time explaining their interest in a new job. The best way to handle a blind ad, if you think it could be your current employer's, is to have a friend answer it, listing the type of qualifications in his query to guarantee a response, if the ad is legitimate. If contacted, your friend excuses himself from consideration by stating he is no longer interested and gives you the company's name and address.

The best way to land a job, however, is through the hidden job market: unadvertised jobs filled by personal contacts and word-of-mouth. As you gain experience and make new contacts in your line of work, you'll get some offers, circumventing all of the conventional methods of finding a job.

ENHANCING YOUR EMPLOYMENT QUALIFICATIONS

◆

Have you ever been barred from a job you knew you could do because of what seemed an unreasonable requirement? Say you applied for an office job similar to those you'd held throughout your career and found this employer required a college degree. You probably would find this requirement unreasonable. Another employer might require five years' experience in a field in which you had four, barring you from consideration despite your skill.

At this point, you would have to consider fudging, or falsifying, your qualifications on the application. However, you must take certain precautions not to get caught. Several spectacular cases of falsifying qualifications for jobs have been revealed in recent years only because the deceptions surfaced...years after the applicants got the jobs and succeeded at them.

In one case, a small Arizona town hired an applicant for chief of police based on his listed qualifications: former Green Beret; graduate of Los Angeles Police Department academy; former officer for the Los Angeles and Compton,

15

California, police departments; worked for Federal Bureau of Investigation, Central Intelligence Agency, and Drug Enforcement Administration. A later charge of police brutality and illegal planting of evidence prompted an extensive investigation into the chief's background, which disclosed that all of his claims were false. The chief had never even graduated from high school. The revealing point is that the Arizona Law Enforcement Officers Advisory Council only spot-checked for law-enforcement certification, investigating only about ten percent of the applicants. If the chief had stayed out of serious trouble, he might have continued undetected indefinitely.

Another, better-publicized case of falsifying qualifications involved Darrow Duke Tully, former publisher of the *Arizona Republic*, a Phoenix newspaper. Tully had claimed for years to have been a U.S. Air Force officer, a fighter pilot with combat experience in Korea and Vietnam. As a reservist, he claimed to have flown on active duty in Vietnam and downed enough enemy planes to become an ace. Tully regularly appeared at parties for retired and reserve Air Force officers dressed in his Air Force lieutenant colonel's dress uniform.

The truth came out in a press conference on 26 December 1985 when Tom Collins, Maricopa County Attorney, disclosed that Tully had never served in the military. Tully and Collins had gotten into a knock-down, drag-out political fight, and Collins, as a matter of routine, ran an extensive background check on Tully. It didn't take much to reveal Tully's lies.

In studying these cases, we have to remember that although these two got caught, they did so only after many years. Surely there are many others who have avoided investigation by keeping a low profile. With a little initiative and judgment, an applicant can falsify his qualifications and remain undetected for years — or forever.

Background Check

The main point to remember about enhancing your qualifications is that most employers (including most governmental agencies) don't carry out thorough background checks if the applicant looks good.

The second point is that any qualification enhancement you attempt must appear credible. For this, remember that it's easier to stretch qualifications than to create them. If you attended college but did not graduate, you can still claim to have earned a degree. If, however, you never attended medical school or worked in the medical field, claiming to be a doctor will be risky because most competent medical workers will detect your lack of experience and skill.

Don't claim to have worked in a field you don't know or understand. You won't have the skills needed, and you won't know the jargon. Not being able to talk like a pro will expose you quickly.

The third main point is the more experienced you are, the less important formal education becomes. A prospective employer will be more interested in what you've accomplished during the last few years than in a degree you earned two decades ago. This means he'll check into your last job or two, but won't bother verifying your education. Employers often assume that a previous employer has already checked the early background.

How To Do It: The Nuts and Bolts

Claiming a degree you don't have will be much easier if you're well-spoken. People tend to equate polished speech with formal education, and if you're articulate, you'll find it easier to convince people you have a degree. In listing your degree, use a college or university you have attended because you might meet someone else who attended, and it helps to be able to recall various instructors, deans, or students in casual conversation.

Stretching your work experience is, believe it or not, even easier. If you're a machinist with four years' experience, and the employer requires five, then correctly list your genuine experience on the application: ABC Machine Co. Hired January 1984. Left January 1988.

Don't try to falsify your hiring date in order to fill out the five years. That's too easy to check with one phone call. Instead, list a fictitious previous employer in another city some distance away. (In most fields, everybody knows everyone else in that particular locale and your prospective employer might know that the company had never existed.) The needed year comes just before your actual employment: XYZ Machine Co. Hired January 1983. Left January 1984.

Under reason for leaving, state that XYZ Machine Company went out of business, giving yourself an excellent reason for leaving after only one year and forestalling any effort to check on your employment at XYZ. If the employer checks with ABC and finds you were a satisfactory employee, he'll probably accept your story.

Listing previous salary is another area in which applicants often choose to fudge. You may wish to claim you were paid more than you actually were as a psychological ploy to ask for more money from a prospective employer. Once you've determined that he's not the type to pay the least amount possible, you can start your program.

Personal appearance is important to presenting an image of a well-paid person. Dressing expensively and driving an expensive car tend to substantiate your salary claims. In some cases you might need supporting paperwork. Just in case, obtain a blank W-2 form from the Internal Revenue Service and fill it out for the previous year's salary using the figure you stated on the job application. Have this ready, but show it only if the interviewer requests it.

Derogatory Information

What if you have something to conceal? Can you cover up the fact that you were fired from a previous job? Yes; your chances are better than ever. Prospective employers now face significant legal restrictions on the types of questions they may ask, and former employers are restricted by even more far-reaching deterrents in what they may reveal about former employees. A prospective employer still may not ask your race, religion, or national origin, for example, but he also can't do as much as before when checking employee backgrounds without resorting to high-priced private investigation.

Years ago, employers could check with each other regarding suitability of employees and former employees. Then came a few lawsuits by former employees who claimed that they had been defamed by negative references. One such case involved a former security officer fired by Mervyn's, a department store chain headquartered in California. He sued and won $280,000 in damages.

To avoid such future lawsuits, employers then developed a code, unwritten and unstated but understood among themselves: if a former employee had done well, he would get positive references; if he'd been fired or performed poorly, the former employer would ignore or refuse to answer any requests for references by him or prospective employers who inquired. Today, with the threat of lawsuits greater than ever, former employers usually will confirm only the time frame during which an employee worked. In some cases, usually with the written permission of the former employee, the employer will reveal salary. Arizona and a few other states have antiblacklisting laws that seriously restrict what a company may reveal about any of its former employees.

From the employer's viewpoint, the threat of lawsuit has become so serious that a hospital in the Midwest refused to reveal that they suspected a former staffer of poisoning patients. Another hospital then hired him. Because the hospital which had previously employed him was afraid of a defamation suit and declined to issue any warning, this person was able to kill another few dozen people before he was caught and prosecuted.

Employers will fight tooth and nail to protect their rights. In some cases, they'll fight employee lawsuits all the way to the U.S. Supreme Court to maintain the upper hand. With more resources to devote to the legal battle, employers usually win. Employees who want to fight often are unable to find a lawyer who will accept their case on a contingency basis since the type of suit is so difficult to win.

Although corporations make every effort to win lawsuits, they take even more precautions to avoid lawsuits. What this means is that you should not worry too much about having been fired. More than likely, your former employer has reasons just as strong as yours to keep that fact secret. On application forms or in interviews, just indicate that you left for more money or a job closer to home, whichever applies better.

PSYCHOLOGICAL PREEMPLOYMENT TESTS

During the 1950s, hustling, fast-talking psychologists sold some employers the idea that, with modern psychological testing, they could find ideal employees for them. These psychologists claimed tests could spot certain psychological types well-suited for specific positions. This idea caught on among larger corporations that could afford the high fees charged for the test, and many job applicants found themselves subjected to inkblot and other types of tests originally designed for mental patients.

After a few years, the bubble burst. Employers began to realize that few, if any, psychological profiles are ideally suited for specific positions, and, even if they were, psychologists weren't doing a good job of matching them. Psychological testing for people outside of clinical settings fell into disrepute for a generation. Now, with new people in charge of the corporations, the pendulum is swinging back.

Why would any employer want to fool around with a science that's mainly charlatanism in order to screen employees? Because good marketing and salesmanship by the companies offering the screening services have convinced yet another generation of business executives who have not learned the lesson of their forerunners.

Psychologists stress the financial angle to businessmen. They assert that psychological screening is less expensive than background investigations. This apparently compelling argument is even winning converts in the nation's police forces (*Law Enforcement News*, 15 April 1988). Predictably, performance usually falls short of promise. It's going to take time for the negative results to become widely known again, and until then, the cycle will continue.

Currently, the sales pitch doesn't promise that the test will find the right psychological type, but rather that it will screen out psychotics, neurotics, alcoholics, drug abusers, and persons inclined to dishonesty. Psychologists specializing in preemployment testing often warn that their test results should be only one factor in the hiring decision. This less-ambitious claim gives psychologists an excuse if the applicant doesn't work out.

Psychological tests don't work any better than they ever did. They're just being marketed more astutely.

Psychological tests can be threatening to the applicant. If you're nervous at the prospect of being tested in a way you don't understand, relax. It's normal to feel anxious when confronted with trick questions and hidden manipulations.

Merely taking the tests causes anxiety, even though the person administering them makes a show of trying to soothe and relax you. Just remember this important point: there's usually no time limit. The tester may announce that the test should take a certain amount of time, and may even tell you to work quickly. He is being deceptive to get you to give impulsive answers instead of thoughtful ones. If the instructions state that you must answer all of the questions, you know that there is no time limit and you can take your time. (Remember this point later in this discussion.)

You may find that the test contains questions that call for true/false answers, and which appear to have no connection with the job you're seeking. The questions may ask whether you smoke or drink, how often you exceed the speed limit when you drive, and what sort of books or movies you like. You may wonder what any of this has to do with your qualifications for the job.

Nothing really, but, according to the psychologists, the answers you give disclose what sort of person you are. Actually, what is revealed by the questions on the test is the way psychologists think about the rest of us. By realizing this, you can get valuable pointers on how to beat the tests.

The first, and possibly most important, point is that nobody's perfect. Various questions relate to both major and minor faults and human problems. Anyone who answers that he never worries about anything, never has sleepless nights, and never gets headaches is obviously not being truthful. Interspersed among the questions about minor shortcomings will be ones meant to reveal major concerns, such as drug abuse and criminal convictions. Scoring the answers involves listing the answers to minor and major points separately. However, in the test itself, the questions are mixed together to confuse you and make it more difficult for you to spot the patterns they will look for in your answers.

Criminal History

Some questionnaires ask outright if you've committed or been convicted of any of a variety of felonies. The rule here is deny, deny, deny! You gain nothing by admitting to a major crime, unless you're on parole or probation and are seeking a job. In such a case, you're usually required to inform your prospective employer of your criminal record and your parole officer of prospective employment. However, even if you're in this situation, absolutely deny having committed any other crimes.

Watch carefully, though, for other questions interspersed in this section. The questions may ask whether you've had loud arguments at work. Arguments aren't criminal, and realistically it's hard to find a person to which this has never happened. If you see this question, consider that it may be part of the lie score.

The Lie Score

The lie score, which estimates the truthfulness of your answers, is crucial to determining whether you pass or fail the test. The answers you give to questions dealing with minor problems and failings add up to determine your lie score. Some questions will ask whether you ever get headaches, argue with your wife, tell lies, or think about committing a crime. Try to paint a believable picture of yourself with your answers. After all, everyone has headaches or lies occasionally. You can even admit to having thought about committing a minor crime at one time or other, but never admit to having thought about doing a major crime, such as rape or robbery. If you admit to that, you'll find it counts heavily against you.

The lie score is often expressed as a percentage value. If you deny more than 25 percent of the minor points, psychologists assume that you are being deceptive. The higher percentage you get on the deception scale, the less likely that your other answers are truthful, according to the psychologists. With some tests, you can detect questions comprising the lie score by turning to the last page and reading the questions in reverse order. Since there's usually no time limit, you can spare a minute or two to do this. If there is a question asking how often you have stolen from your employer, except for minor office supplies, that's your tip-off. It's all right to admit to having taken pens and pencils in earlier questions in the test. Likewise, if you find a question relating to how much money you devote to drugs, and the question specifically excludes alcohol or cigarettes, that's also a clue to help you answer questions which will come up earlier in the test concerning alcohol or smoking.

Another subtle point, if the test is computer-scored, is that the number of damaging answers you admit to tends to hold down your lie score. If, for example, you admit to having a bad driving record or even to an arrest for drunk driving, this damaging admission will place you in a very truthful category.

Psychologists assume if you tell the truth about small matters, you also will tell the truth about important ones. This is why, if your lie score is within acceptable limits, they'll usually accept your total score.

Measuring Attitudes

Another category you'll find on these tests pertains to alcohol and drug use. The questions won't ask directly if you have an alcohol or drug problem. Instead, they prefer to address the topic deviously by asking if your friends drink or use drugs. You may also be asked if you favor stronger penalties for drunk driving and drug use. These questions can take diverse forms. Some may ask directly if you ever drink or take recreational drugs while at work. Another question may ask if you ever drink or take illegal drugs at social gatherings.

It's all right to admit to drinking socially. In fact, it's

best not to deny this unless you abstain for religious or medical reasons. But never admit to taking any illegal drugs or drinking on the job under any circumstances.

Other questions may ask if you know many people who drink alcohol. You may be asked to check a percentage range, such as 10 to 20 percent. Always check the middle range on this type of question. On the part about illegal drugs, always check off the lowest percentage. Admitting that you are acquainted with many dopers is, in the minds of the people who designed these tests, guilt by association.

You'll also find questions relating to stealing and employee honesty. You may be asked if you have ever stolen anything, even paper or pens. This is possibly the only question to which you can answer yes without risk of failing the test. Since these tests supposedly measure honesty by measuring attitudes, the rest of your answers should reflect a hard-line approach to employee honesty. When asked if you think all or most people steal from their employers, answer no. If asked whether employers should fire or prosecute people who steal from them, answer yes. Don't make the mistake of excusing a thief.

Some tests may question whether you would ever steal in certain hypothetical cases. Clearly, admitting that you might steal from your employer at some future date—under any circumstances—will count heavily against you.

The most subtle questions pertain to attitudes towards employers. Likely questions regard whether you think some employers mistreat their employees or make excessive profits, either legally or illegally, by taking advantage of their positions, and whether some employees are justified in cheating their employers. To all of these, you must answer negatively because to admit to any of these attitudes, however realistic they are, is interpreted as favoring theft.

Another set of questions may deal with whether you know or have ever known anyone dishonest. The proper answers to these are either no or few. If asked whether or not you ever thought of stealing something, you can answer yes for minor items, because as stated, these are likely to be part of the lie score. Never admit to thinking about taking any large items or embezzling money.

The simplistic assumption behind these questions is that the straight-arrow person sought by employers doesn't steal or use drugs and doesn't associate with anyone who does. The ideal employee, according to the assumption, also believes that most people, especially employers, are fair and honest. The ideal candidate will express a harsh and punitive attitude towards those who steal or use drugs. To convince the psychologists that you're upright, honest, and free of any addictions, you must answer that you strongly disapprove of illegal drugs, excessive alcohol consumption, and stealing in any form. Emphasize that your friends share these values, and you believe thieves and dopers should be punished to the fullest extent of the law.

You may be asked about mandatory drug testing in the workplace; if so, indicate that you think an employer has the right to demand it from his employees. If you really want to score points, state that any employee who refuses to take a drug test should be fired. Likewise, if you find a question dealing with the company's right to search employees suspected of theft, you're safer if you answer that they should search suspects.

From this outline, it appears that employers are seeking the type of person who isn't too bright, doesn't question authority, and walks a straight-and-narrow path. This personality type best fits menial or service jobs, which is what the tests reflect. As one psychologist put it, the tests are designed for the meat-and-potatoes type of person. This sort of person drinks beer (moderately) and watches the game in his free time instead of reading a book, for instance.

If you're applying for that type of job, you can tailor your answers to fit what they're looking for. The designers of these tests don't give the rest of us any credit for subtlety because they assume we can't spot the tricks. Psychologists also don't seem to realize that many people can and do lie successfully in job interviews. People who know how to lie convincingly tell modest, believable lies. Skilled liars can figure out the tests without coaching.

It's not necessary to be a professional or experienced liar to pass the tests, once you know the tricks. One strategy you can adopt is the sacrifice plan. For example, if you know that the job you're seeking does not involve any driving on company business, and you have something else to hide, admit to a drunk-driving arrest, even if it's false. This will push down your lie score and you can deny something else with much less risk of being challenged. As we've learned, employers are often suspicious about the assets prospective employees claim and carefully check them out; but they assume that any damaging admission must be true and the person must be truthful to have made it. If the employer runs a background check on you and examination of court records fails to turn up any drunk-driving conviction, he will probably assume the records got screwed up.

Inkblot Tests

Inkblot tests are totally unsuited for preemployment screening, but some psychologists insist on using them anyway. They can be trickier than other tests because seemingly innocent answers can count against you. Your strategy in defeating an inkblot test involves two principles:

1) Avoid answers that suggest any mental disorder to the psychologist. Don't give any blood-and-guts responses (such as intestines and other anatomical details); answers that suggest paranoia (such as eyes watching you); descriptions dependent on color (such as drops of blood); or cloud responses, which often are interpreted as signs of anxiety (one exception is the mushroom-cloud response since nuclear bombs are a fact of life today). People and animals, as long as the inkblots resemble them, are safe, normal answers.

2) Give job-related answers when possible to interfere with the numerical scoring system used to interpret the responses. Psychologists consider job-related answers insignificant and discount them, which reduces the significance of other responses. Describing plumbing fixtures, mechanical parts, and other items encountered on the job would not count against you if you were applying for a job as a plumber. Neither does a butcher's animal-carcass response.

Now that you've passed the written and association tests, you have to tackle the screening interview. It can be easy if you know the sort of answers they're seeking from applicants. However, in some cases, before you meet with anyone, you may have to pass another ordeal: the lie-detector test.

THE POLYGRAPH

The polygraph, or lie-detector test, is a piece of technological chicanery sometimes substituted for a background check in employee screening. The reason? It's cheaper.

Checking out an applicant's background involves contacting his former employers and interviewing his friends and neighbors. It takes a lot of time and money. Some government agencies do this before granting a security clearance, but the government has the resources to spend on a comprehensive security investigation. After all, the government doesn't have to show a profit at year's end. A private employer does, so he often tries to pare even nickels and dimes from operating expenses. Combined with the expense of private investigations is the reluctance of past employers to provide any derogatory information about former employees. So private employers often succumb to the sales pitch of polygraph operators who claim they can save them the expense of background investigations.

Federal law has severely restricted private employers'

use of polygraphs. Jobseekers are now far less likely to face the abuses that used to be mandatory. Still, it's helpful to have a working knowledge of the hardware and the techniques just in case. If you apply for any position that involves public safety, you may be required to take a polygraph test. You may also encounter polygraph testing after you've accepted a position.

The Polygraph: History and Theory

Invented in the early 1920s, the polygraph has not been improved much since. Not long after its invention, the machine and its operators proved too inaccurate to be used in court, a point few polygraph operators bring up unless asked. Some operators even try to make the polygraph appear legitimate by stating that polygraph evidence can be introduced in certain states with the consent of both parties.

If it were possible to determine a suspect's guilt or innocence by hooking him up to a machine, it would unclog our crowded court calendars and eliminate doubts about jury verdicts. However, the polygraph has several serious shortcomings, primarily the assumption behind its design.

The polygraph operates on the theory that a person telling a lie will experience stress, manifested by irregular breathing, increased heart rate and blood pressure, and increased sweating, which lowers the conductivity of the skin. A set of pens on the polygraph records changes in heart and breathing rate, blood pressure, and skin conductivity. By reading the changes, the polygraph operator is supposed to be able to tell when the subject is lying.

This theory has several weaknesses, as Burt Rapp points out in his book, *Interrogation* (Loompanics, 1987). The obvious one is that most people who undergo a polygraph examination are tense and anxious because jobseeking is stressful. Another factor not taken into consideration is the accusatory nature of the questions and the presumption that you wouldn't tell the truth without being on the polygraph. Being asked if you have ever used illegal drugs is anxiety-provoking. A series of such questions is likely to raise the blood pressure of most people. Those being tested get particularly anxious when polygraph technicians ask probing questions that have nothing to do with qualification for employment. Some of these technicians are intellectual Peeping Toms, and take advantage of their positions to ask questions regarding sexual habits.

Designers of the polygraph failed to consider another point: not all liars feel or exhibit anxiety. Some people enjoy telling lies. They actually look forward to outwitting someone else. These personality types make good salesmen because they lie easily, without any signs of nervousness. These people make good used-car salesmen. They also sell water softeners and vacuum cleaners door-to-door. They can pass a polygraph examination easily.

Intimidation

Polygraph operators sometimes boast that they obtain confessions even before hooking a subject up to the black box. They do this by intimidation. The naive or ignorant subject who believes everything the operator tells him will accept that the machine is infallible and that he has no chance of getting away with a deception. Some technicians will try to unnerve a subject by tricking him into believing the lie detector is unbeatable. He will tell the subject to pick a card from a deck of playing cards, then ask, "Is your card a heart?" The subject who answers negatively will find the technician shaking his head and telling him that the machine spotted the deception. Actually, all of the cards in the deck are hearts. The operator has succeeded in flustering the subject, hoping to affect his subsequent answers.

How to Pass a Polygraph Test

What are your chances of passing the lie box? There are two things you have to do to pass. The first is to show a lie response when the technician instructs you to lie. The other is not to show a lie response when you being untruthful about an important question.

At the beginning of the test, the technician will calibrate his machine to your responses. To do this, he'll observe your responses when you're telling the truth and when you're not. He'll ask you a series of questions and tell you to answer yes or no to each one. Some sample questions might be:

"Is your name John Smith?"

"Are you in the United States?"

"Are you in China?"

"Are you 39 years old?"

"Do you live at 999 Grove Street?"

These questions enable the technician to see how your responses record on his charts when you're telling the truth and lying. Polygraph technicians know that some people do not record higher responses when they lie, and this preliminary test is to find these people. To pass, you follow the technician's instructions and answer yes or no to every question, as he directs. However, you must increase your stress responses to the questions which obviously are untrue. Hold your breath and tighten the muscles in your buttocks when your answer is untruthful. Or you might try a thumbtack in your shoe, simply pressing your toe down on it when you want to appear to be lying. These will send the needles soaring, and reassure the technician that your reactions are normal.

You must also learn to control your responses when you are lying. One way to train yourself to do this is by using biofeedback equipment. These measure one or more of the same responses as the polygraph, and they show you when your responses are elevated. A few practice sessions will help you verbalize these topics without excessive physiological responses.

Another way to control your responses is by practicing relaxation exercises. Several popular books available at most libraries and bookstores contain methods of relaxing so that your physiological responses stay on an even keel.

Yet another way is psychological desensitization. For this, you need a close, trusted friend with whom you can discuss personal topics freely. Tell him or her about the problems that a polygraph examination may uncover, such as being fired from a job or having stolen from an employer. By repetition, you can desensitize yourself and lower your physiological response to a stressful topic.

One last method you might consider is the fictionalized stress response. If, for example, you are asked if you were ever fired from a job, you can answer yes—even though you haven't been. Whatever your response on the polygraph chart may be, the technician will never interpret this as a lie. People don't generally lie to make themselves look worse. If you register as deceptive the technician will simply interpret this as a result of the emotional stress of being fired. He'll make a note to ask you about it later.

The technician will then move to the actual test. In this, he'll ask you questions such as:

"Have you answered all questions on the application truthfully?"

"Have you ever, apart from the instance you've disclosed, been fired from a job?"

"Have you ever, apart from the instance you've disclosed, been arrested for a crime?"

"Have you ever committed any sexual perversions?" (optional).

"Have you answered all of the questions I've asked you truthfully?"

He'll read the questions to you first and ask you if you understand them. Then he'll hook you up to the box again and ask you each question slowly and deliberately, allowing time between them for your responses to register.

In theory, you have to show a truthful response pattern on the chart to go along with your answers. However, as we'll see, this doesn't mean much in the larger sense because polygraph operators are the biggest liars of all.

The post-test questioning is the next part of the session, and possibly the worst. At this point, the technician will ask you about some apparently troublesome areas in your responses. For example:

"I'm having a problem with your response when you said you'd never been fired from a job. Was that the absolute truth?"

It doesn't matter what the response on his chart reads. The technician is fishing, relying on intimidation to try to squeeze a damaging admission out of you. He knows you can't interpret the squiggles on the chart, and he wouldn't show them to you if you could. He just suggests that you may have been untruthful, feeding your anxiety. He is counting on your wanting or needing the job enough to stand for his emotional bullying. He is bluffing.

If you have never been fired from any job, stand pat. Just tell him that you can't understand how that could be, because you've never been fired. Never, under any circumstances, suggest that either he or his machine could be mistaken or defective. Scientifically, you're probably right, but the hard reality is that he can punish you severely for such an insult to his ability. Be modest, be cool, and, above all, be respectful.

One way to finesse your way around a questionable response is to have a cover story prepared. One man, being tested as a prerequisite for a sensitive federal security position, tried to hide the fact that he was an alcoholic. The technician became suspicious by the applicant's response to alcohol-related questions. When the technician asked him to explain why his graph showed a strong response to questions regarding alcohol, the man pulled out a letter from a relative in another city that informed him that his father had just died of liver disease brought on by excessive drinking. This satisfied the technician, and he got the job. The man drank on the security job, and it took years for his superiors to catch him because the polygraph had cleared him at the outset.

Another way to outwit the box when you have something to hide might be to make a damaging admission against yourself, but one less serious than what you're trying to hide. For example, if you were fired from a previous job for stealing, admit that you were fired, but don't give the real reason for your dismissal. Don't insist that your boss was wrong in firing you or try to excuse your behavior. Instead, claim that he fired you because he caught you in an illicit liaison with his wife.

"I was just a kid. The boss was 55 and she was 27. She kept making passes at me, and one thing led to another because I was attracted to her, too. He played golf every afternoon during the summer, and one day he returned early after his golf partner failed to show and caught his wife and me together in the office with the doors locked. We managed to get dressed by the time he got the door open, but he knew what we'd been doing. That was it. I was fired."

The technician won't question this version too closely, and your prospective employer probably won't telephone your former employer to find out the details about his wife's affair with you. Even if he does, he won't be surprised if your former employer denies the alleged incident with his wife. Few people would admit something this personal to a stranger who telephones. This version for your firing is much less incriminating than admitting to tapping the till because your former employer was underpaying you.

Internal Security

Internal security investigations, such as for thefts or information leaks, provide an excuse for a more sinister application of the lie detector. Too often these become fishing expeditions to dredge up information unconnected with the actual investigation. Although it's true that you don't have to take the test, your employer doesn't have to retain you in your job, either. He has subtle ways of letting you know that the road to promotion is by agreeing to cooperate with the investigation.

This places you in a dilemma. If there's an accusation of dishonesty spread among several employees, and the employer wants to use the lie detector to cut down the odds, you're in double danger. You may stand falsely accused if you fail to pass the test, and you also risk being coerced into accusing another employee. This is the dirty underside of polygraph testing that technicians don't like to discuss. After the round of questions relating to your possible participation in the alleged theft, you'll hear questions such as these:

"Do you know of anyone who had anything to do with

the theft?"

"Do you suspect anyone of having done it?"

"Do you know any employee who has taken anything in the past?"

"Do you know any employee who has taken anything from a former employer?"

"Has any other employee told you that he or she suspects anyone of the theft?"

"Has any other employee, to your knowledge, done anything disloyal to the company?"

"Do you suspect any other employee of having done anything disloyal to the company?"

"Has any employee told you of doing anything disloyal to the company?"

"Do you know of any employee who has been disloyal to this company or a former employer?"

The technician has designed these questions as cross-checks, and you can be sure that other employees will face similar questions. An important aspect of this type of investigation is secrecy. The technician will state, at the beginning or at the end, that the investigation is confidential and everything you reveal remains between yourself and the company. Likewise, he will stress that you are not to talk about what was discussed in the examination room with other employees. To enforce this, any subsequent lie detector test will have a question asking whether you discussed the previous one with anyone else.

You won't find the same practices in every industry, fortunately. Some labor unions won't allow management to be too aggressive in ferreting out suspicions of employee misconduct. Some employers use more ethical means to seek solid evidence instead of unfounded suspicions.

How They Rate You

Before we leave polygraphs, you must understand one final, yet essential, point: what all those lines mean. There are two schools of thought regarding interpretation of the scores. One claims the squiggles on the chart are everything, and that a competent polygraph operator would be able to interpret a chart without ever seeing the subject. Called blind scoring, this philosophy implies that well-trained, competent polygraph technicians should draw the same conclusions from examining the same chart. This theory hardly ever works in practice.

The other viewpoint relies on global scoring, or considering everything about the subject in determining his truthfulness. This type of operator believes that behavior during the test can be just as revealing as the actual answers. He will interpret your arriving late for or missing an appointment as reluctance to take the test, therefore he assumes you have something to hide. Any signs of bad attitude or noncooperation on your part may be viewed as indications of deception.

So, whenever taking a polygraph examination or even a psychological test, always be aware that the person administering it may use global scoring. Behave respectfully, as you would in an ordinary interview. Be polite, but don't give anything away unnecessarily. The same principle also applies during the interview, which we'll now explore.

THE INTERVIEW

An interview may not seem threatening, but it can make or break your chances of getting the job. The interviewer probably will have a strong faith in his ability to appraise an individual during the interview, and usually the interview is the deciding factor in the hiring decision. Carefully controlled tests, however, have proven that interviews can be terribly misleading. In one test, a panel of interviewers rated a group of applicants who varied from clergymen to convicted felons, and their judgments often were incredibly wrong. Still, most employers rely on interviews.

Intuitively, you already know how to behave in an interview. You must be prompt, neat, clean, cheerful, cooperative, and polite. You have to seem open and honest, and do or say nothing to antagonize the interviewer.

Understand at the outset that there are two types of interviews: structured and unstructured. In the structured interview, the interviewer asks you a series of questions about your experience, education, and other factors that bear upon your suitability for the job. Many questions will try to get you to bring out more information than you listed in your résumé or application. This fairly straightforward type of interview allows the employer to get a fuller picture of your experience and ability. Note, however, that although the interview is structured, the questions will be such that you'll have to organize an answer, not reply with a yes or no. The interviewer will be interested in how you put together your answers and how coherent and relevant they are.

The unstructured interview is quite different; it is used by those who like to play games with other people's minds. The interviewer does not lead off with direct questions, but only general and open-ended ones such as, "Tell me about yourself." If you lose your poise at this point, you'll fail. You must not respond with, "What do you want to know?" or show any signs of confusion or uncertainty.

One question often encountered relates to your hobbies and recreational activities. If the interviewer asks about your hobbies, never mention any solitary ones, such as reading. Always mention those that involve a group, such as softball or bowling. He's looking for people who appear comfortable and eager to work with others.

One good way to handle this sort of question is by repeating the information you've already supplied in your résumé or application. You should stick to this safe way unless interrupted with specific questions.

It also helps to understand the interviewer's mind-set. Some interviewers believe that an innocent person will have a harsher, more punitive attitude towards a lawbreaker than a guilty one would. They use this to try to uncover those who would steal from the company. They might ask a question such as what should happen to someone who steals from his employer? They'll have more confidence in the person who answers send them to jail than one who suggests maybe he needed the money. Anyone who seems to excuse a hypothetically guilty party reveals himself as potentially guilty himself. The simpleminded assumption here is like the one operating in the written tests. To give an impression of unquestionable honesty it's necessary to display an uncompromisingly punitive attitude towards anyone who would steal from his employer.

In his book, *Knock 'em Dead*, Martin John Yate stresses the importance of maintaining one's poise during the interview. Interviewers try to trip you up with confusing or tricky questions; just remember it's more important to retain your poise than to give a thoroughly studied answer.

Be prepared for a few tricks. One type of interviewer will stare at you after you've finished, not saying anything, trying to make you nervous. You should wait calmly and smile, or prompt him by asking if there is anything else he would like to know.

The interviewer may try to trap you with a couple of questions that seem straightforward, but contain hidden dangers. One is asking you to describe your greatest weakness. This is really a Catch-22, because if you deny having any weaknesses, you'll obviously be lying. If you answer truthfully, you'll be handing the interviewer something to use against you. The solution is, frankly, a fast shuffle. You could reply that you find it frustrating to have to work with other employees who aren't doing their best for the company.

If asked what you didn't like about your last job, or what you thought of your last employer, recognize this as a trap. About the job, you can answer that it wasn't challenging enough. Regarding your employer, always reply that you got along well with him and you found him to be a fair person, or some such nonsense. The interviewer will be listening carefully to your answer, alert for signs of anyone who might be a disgruntled employee. You don't want to criticize your last employer, or any former employer, because a future employer is looking for signals that might indicate potential malcontents.

Another ploy used by interviewers who like to play mind games is to repeat a phrase from your last answer, then stare at you. If, for example, you answered this way, "Yes, in my last job I had total responsibility for ordering paper towels," the interviewer might say, "Total responsibility?" in a questioning way, then wait for your reply. You should simply repeat, "Yes, total responsibility," with assurance and wait for the next question. If you allow the interviewer to intimidate you into expanding upon or justifying your use of the word total, you'll appear uncertain of yourself and you may end up saying more than you intended.

Some people in charge of filling jobs rely on the stress interview, designed to make you lose your cool. The interviewer might say something like, "I'm not sure you're qualified for this job." Don't react to the statement; don't blush, get angry, or start describing your experience and qualifications again. You might ask the interviewer why he thinks that. Or you might remark that if he were convinced of that, he probably would not have spent so much time with you. You'll soon find out if this was a sincere dismissal or just a ploy to draw a response.

Always remember that those who play these mind games do it for their own gratification. They need to feel superior to the applicant. This may take some petty forms. If, for example, you're well-dressed and driving an expensive car, the interviewer might ask if your car is car paid for. Answer no, even if you paid cash for it. Give him his little victory.

Don't let yourself get caught off guard by a hidden or

disguised interview. The personnel officer may end the interview, and then invite you for lunch or a cup of coffee. During this informal meeting, he'll try to find out more about you. You won't know what he's looking for, unless you know someone working in that company who can inform you. The interviewer may be interested in your religious beliefs or political coloration. He might want to know your stance on a specific or controversial issue, such as gun control or abortion.

One pitfall you definitely should avoid is accepting an alcoholic drink at lunch. Some employers consider alcohol a serious problem and avoid hiring any candidate who drinks excessively. The interviewer may consider anyone who has a drink with lunch to be an alcohol abuser. Refusing a drink is much easier today because of the emphasis on suppression of drunk driving. You simply can reply, "No, thanks, I'm driving." Use this excuse even if you came to the interview by public transportation. You can always say that you have to drive later in the day.

Be careful what you give away in casual conversation. You have to walk a delicate line between keeping up your end of a light conversation and stubbornly clamming up. If the interviewer turns the subject to politics, you can answer noncommittally by saying that you read something about that subject in the newspaper that morning or by nodding your head if that will satisfy him. A safe answer is "You may be right," or, "I see what you mean." It's good practice never to get into any sort of argument or disagreement with the interviewer.

In answer to a direct question, you might reply that you're uncertain because you haven't read enough about the subject. You might also say that you just don't know. Never try to be too clever and answer a question with a question.

This may annoy the person on whose goodwill you depend.

Both employers and police officers get the most damaging admissions from nervous people who volunteer information. As we've seen, this is the purpose behind the unstructured interview. In a casual setting, such as conversation over lunch, it's much harder to be on your guard, but you must remain more watchful than ever. The interviewer may try to entice an admission from you by saying, "I was once at a party where they used cocaine." This is a trap. If you deny ever knowing anyone who used drugs, you may strain his credulity. On the other hand, if you tell him that you attend dope-laced parties every weekend, you'll talk yourself right out of the job. A good compromise answer might be, "That's interesting. I never was at a dope party myself, but a guy in one of my college classes smoked marijuana."

The exact topics of concern to employers vary according to the area of the country, the type of employment, and the type of company. In some locales, you should not admit that you're not a regular churchgoer. In other areas, almost anything goes.

Sometimes, you just can't win. If the interviewer has a hidden agenda, or is judging you by unconventional criteria, you can do little to influence his decision. For example, personnel officers for one major department store chain would take candidates for executive positions to lunch just to see if they salted their food before tasting it. Those who salted their food first weren't hired.

In some cases, the interviewer is trying to decide if you are a headstrong person who is likely to provoke arguments on the job. This sort of interviewer will listen carefully to your answers, looking for signs of irritation. He may discuss any topic at all, just to get a rise out of you, then contradict you to find out how you react. Never pursue a topic too far, and never try to win an argument with an interviewer. You may win the battle, but you'll lose the war.

THE WORKPLACE

Now that you've got the job, let's look at the hazards and opportunities it could present. Some jobs provide better opportunities for working the angles than others. Similarly, some employers deserve to be robbed blind because of the way they treat their employees.

You have to decide for yourself because it's impossible to generalize. Does your employer treat you fairly? Is he the sort of person you'd want for a friend? If so, you probably want to walk the straight and narrow at work and be as fair as you can to the person who treats you right.

On the other hand, do you think your employer is exploiting you? Did he or she hire you at an unfairly low wage because you were desperate for a job? Have you been refused promotions or raises even though you've done an outstanding job for the company? Does he exploit all of his employees? Does your employer make pie-in-the-sky promises that he never keeps? Does he give all the good jobs to his relatives, while leaving the dirty details to you and others he hired off the street? If so, then you need to get back some of what's yours.

In most cases, you won't get it by joining a union. Many unions exist not so much to help the employees, but to collect dues to pay the fat salaries of union officials. In many cases, they have sold out the people they represent by signing sweetheart contracts with the employer.

You have to look out for yourself. You do this by staying alert and aware, ever watchful for the opportunity to make a few extra bucks. In this, you have to be cautious and make the most of opportunities that come your way. You also have to know how to create opportunities for yourself.

All You Can Steal

In your workplace, don't even make off with a pen or paper clip until you know the ropes. You need to know what's under tight control and what isn't. You need to know what will be missed and what won't. Most of all, you need to know what is worth taking.

It might surprise you to know you can take many items without stealing them. One national company changed over from one brand of copy machine to another. The salesman had told them that paper for the old machines wouldn't work in the new ones, and company officials had the entire stock, worth hundreds of dollars, thrown in the trash. Alert employees recovered many reams of paper, which were still useful for typing letters, writing notes, and other uses.

Making off with merchandise is becoming more difficult. Modern inventory-keeping systems maintain detailed records of every item in stock, making it risky to remove anything without the loss being noticed. However, every system has its weaknesses; no inventory-keeping system, no matter how well computerized, is 100-percent fail-safe. Human error, or more precisely, an accumulation of human errors, makes any system vulnerable. This is why businesses take inventory every year to reconcile the records with the physical count, even if they have to close for a few days to do it.

At inventory time, items that should be there may not be, while others that aren't on any lists suddenly appear. These unaccounted for items present an interesting possibility if you're involved in the physical count. It's easy to take something that no one knows about because it won't be missed at inventory time.

You should avoid certain ways of attempting to steal because they're too public. One is accepting gratuities from a salesman. If you're a department head, purchasing agent, or have other discretionary authority, you'll find salesmen asking you to lunch, bringing you gifts, and sending you tickets to a ball game. Of course, these gifts aren't sent because of your sparkling wit or charming personality, but simply to influence your buying decisions. If you accept anything at all, you'll provide justification for rumors that you're on the take.

Some companies have strict policies regarding gratuities. They forbid employees from accepting anything, even a pen and pencil set, no matter how little the cash value. Other companies have more relaxed rules, allowing lunches, desk sets, and other fairly nominal gifts. If you set policy for your department, you should adopt a hard-line stance and stick to it. Anything else makes you vulnerable.

In many cases, what is most available and most beneficial to you is free for the taking. This is information. In some cases, an employer will try to hire you cheaply, but will also provide you with the opportunity to learn. This is your cue to learn all you can and use it to qualify for a better job. If the employer has a benefit package that includes reimbursed education, exploit it to the fullest, whether you want to remain with the company or not.

Another way to benefit from your job is to make copies of computer programs. Many companies use personal computers with over-the-counter programs, such as word processing, data base, and spreadsheet programs, which are worth money to others who don't have them. All of these come on discs, and most can be copied onto blank discs. Only a few programs are copy-protected. Manufacturers have found that most consumers want to make a working disc to use and save the original disc as a backup in case anything happens to the working disc. They also have found that the copy-protecting devices, which cost extra, don't work against determined computer hackers.

Using Inside Information

Perhaps the most lucrative use of information is in the insider field. Some occupations give you an inside view of developments in the business world that you can exploit to earn money with no pain or strain. For example, if you work for a bank, you may have an inside view of which companies are going to do well or poorly in the stock market during the next few months. This insider information can be quite beneficial.

One large bank has a code of ethics booklet which it issues to every new employee. One of the rules states that the employee will not use information acquired on the job for personal benefit. The restriction is hypocritical, of course, because this is precisely how top executives acquire their personal wealth. They feel free to use insider information themselves, but don't want the lower echelons to share the wealth.

One important reason executives don't want to share

information is that when they discover a certain company will be doing well in the near future, they buy its stock while the price is still low. If many people are trying to buy the same stock, the price goes up and the top people can't pick it up as cheaply, which cuts into their profit when they ultimately sell their shares.

How can you benefit from insider information? First you have to be in the right place at the right time. One good slot is in the production planning or purchasing department of a large company, giving you a preview of contracts to be awarded in the near future. If any contracts are going to publicly owned companies that aren't doing well on the stock market, you have the opportunity to buy shares low and sell them after their price rises when news of the contract becomes public knowledge.

Being in government service can provide valuable inside information. If you work for one of the government's procurement agencies, you may have access to the sort of information that you'll be able to exploit for profit.

A word of warning, however. There are laws against such practices. If you're in a sensitive position, your stock portfolio, as well as other aspects of your personal finances, will be under close scrutiny. You may be required to file financial disclosure forms with your employer. Any tangible benefit you derive from insider information will be documented and subjected to investigation.

On 30 August 1988, Associated Press ran an article on what can happen to those who use insider information for personal enrichment. The story revealed that three leading brokerage houses —Prudential-Bache Securities, Inc.; Merrill Lynch; and Advest of Hartford, Connecticut—had fired brokers in connection with a scandal involving advance information leaked from *Business Week* magazine. The article went on to state that authorities believed employees of the company that printed *Business Week* leaked the information to the brokers, who then traded it on that basis.

What's significant about this case is the amount of money involved was too small to be worth mentioning in the article. Clearly, the people caught with their ethics hanging out were low-level employees of these giant brokerage firms. They were quickly sacrificed, which is why you must not get caught trying to do what the big boys do.

One way to avoid this is to have a distant relative or friend do the investing for you. It can't be your wife, because in many cases wives' finances also come under the microscope. The safest system uses a friend in a different field (one who isn't easily identified with you), with whom you trade information. You earn money based on information he passes to you, and vice versa. If you're certain not to leave a paper trail, you can't get caught because you don't have access to the information you'd need to select investments in an unrelated field.

Fringe Benefits

Companies provide many perquisites and other fringe benefits. Some are expressly intended to compensate high-level executives in nontaxable ways and are denied to the rank and file. Others are merely reimbursement for expenses, but if you're smart you can manipulate the system to get a little extra for yourself.

One frequent benefit is reimbursement for miles driven in your personal car. If you regularly drive on business, you can exploit this in one of two ways. The first works only if you have a permissive comptroller, or if the person who disburses the petty cash allows it. Simply put in for more miles than you actually drove. If you have to specify where you went, don't inflate it by much. On the other hand, if you don't have to itemize, you can get away with a lot. The second way, which works even with strictly itemized receipts, is by listing a fictitious trip. You put down the correct mileage, but don't go. Another way to work this is to go to a specific place, but write a slip for travel to another place much farther away.

Reimbursement for meals can be another potential source of extra compensation. Collect receipts from your wife and friends and turn them in. Of course, they should not be dated receipts, as these might reveal an inconsistency. Another way is to use the breakfast chit. You eat breakfast at home and stop at a diner or donut shop for a cup of coffee. Make sure this establishment uses only handwritten receipts. If you collect one for fifty cents, you write in a three to make it read three dollars and fifty cents.

Education is another frequent fringe benefit. Some companies pay for their employees' education directly or by reimbursement. Some employers will pay only for job-related training, while others pay for any courses. If your employer offers educational benefits, take them. They're free and often can help you qualify for a better job with your present employer or a future one. If you decide to change jobs, you take your education with you.

DEFENDING YOURSELF AGAINST THE POST OFFICE

For the past twenty-five years, postal rates have gone up while the quality of service has gone down. The recent postal rate hike to twenty-five cents for a first-class letter coincided with a drop in the number of hours service windows are open and the deterioration of local deliveries. Mail comes later in the day, and it's addressed to someone else much more frequently. Worse, some of your mail, including important envelopes, winds up elsewhere.

Always keep in mind that most of the deterioration in service is not the mail carrier's fault. A carrier is on the bottom of the totem pole and can only obey orders; he doesn't set policy. The higher executives in the post office set the hours carriers work, the routes they follow, and their workloads. If your mail is late because your route carrier is cruelly overworked, the fault belongs to his bosses. What you have to do is defend yourself, not take reprisals against a person who may be as much a victim as yourself.

Save Money on Postage

If you'd like to mail packages cut rate, take advantage of the new postage stamps constantly being issued. Note that the Margaret Mitchell one-cent stamp has a one on it as large as that on the one-dollar stamps, but that the post office has not put a cent sign after it. Note also that the Lilian M. Gilbreth forty-cent stamp has digits much smaller than the one on the Mitchell stamp. If you have a piece of mail requiring more than one dollar postage, use a Mitchell stamp that costs only one cent. Harried postal clerks will mistake it for a dollar stamp most of the time. The worst that can happen to you is your envelope will be returned for more postage. This happens rarely, however, because if a postal clerk does spot it, he'll usually send it on to the addressee with a postage-due notice on it. So if you have to send something to a company that requires more than a simple first-class stamp, put insufficient postage on it. The addressee will have to pay the postage due. This works wherever the addressee may be.

Free Postage

Getting free postage from the Postal Service is easy. This is because the post office customarily returns any envelopes mailed without postage, but they'll forward those with insufficient postage to the addressee to collect the balance. By knowing this policy, you can take advantage of the system.

When mailing a letter to someone in the same city, address it to yourself and use your addressee's address as the return. The postal clerks will mark it RETURNED FOR POSTAGE and send it to the return address. This can only work when addressed to someone in the same city, as even the stupidest postal clerk might have trouble believing that a letter from someone in San Diego got mailed in Des Moines.

Recycling postage stamps is slightly more troublesome and requires a number of like-minded people to work. The post office will reject any letter that has stamps covered by clear tape because this prevents proper cancellation, which would allow users to remove the tape and reuse the stamps. You can prevent stamps from being cancelled and reuse them, however. For this you need a solution of sodium silicate, also known as water glass. You can find this in a child's chemistry set or at a chemical supply house. Chemical suppliers usually sell it in pound bottles, more than enough for ten lifetimes. You don't need this much so buy yours from a hobby-supply store, which carries it in various smaller sizes.

To use the sodium silicate, place your stamps on the envelope in the ordinary way. Then brush on a light coat of water glass solution. The person who gets your letter soaks the envelope in water, which dissolves the coating and the glue. The postmark, of course, goes with the glue. The next step is to reuse the stamp, applying it with ordinary mucilage, the kind that dissolves easily in water. When you get such a treated stamp, you do the same, saving yourself the cost of mailing your next letter.

Junk Mail

No treatment of the postal system would be complete without a discussion of junk mail, which has become more prevalent and more obnoxious in recent years. Junk mail stuffs your mailbox, squeezing out legitimate mail and mutilating magazine covers in the tight fit. The volume of junk mail adds to the carrier's workload and increases his chances of making an error. Junk mail also costs you money; your first-class postage subsidizes junk mailers who use special bulk rates.

You can often spot junk mail by the CAR-RT-SORT code above your name on the address label. This code means that piece has been sent at a special low rate, actually lower than the cost of delivery. You're subsidizing junk mailers by paying higher rates when you mail letters.

Added to the annoyance of having to pay for the privilege of getting junk mail are the devious ways in which junk-mail operators try to get your attention. Today, most people routinely discard gaudy envelopes, which direct-mail companies used to favor to capture your eye. As consumers become more sophisticated in recognizing and discarding junk mail, advertisers have to be more clever—and deceptive. They send their junk mail in tan envelopes designed to look like government mail. Some operators use window envelopes, showing just a glimpse of what looks like a check tucked inside. When you open it, you find that it's merely a voucher for a prize that you can claim only if you go to some resort and attend a demonstration or sales pitch. Another variation is the check that is redeemable for cash only if you buy a big-ticket item, such as a cruise. You pay thousands of dollars for a five-day cruise, and you get twenty-five dollars in spending money. These are rip-offs, but they've done what they were intended to do. They made you open the envelope and read the contents instead of simply throwing it in the trash.

You have several options with which to fight these people without breaking any laws. The simplest way is to look for a business return envelope. This has the postage already paid by the addressee. Seal it and drop it in the mail. The post office will deliver it, empty or not. The junk mail operator will have to pay the freight, which is more than first-class postage.

In some cases, the junk mailer does not include an envelope, but a folder with the business return printed on it. Your name and address are printed on the other side. You may hesitate to return this unless you can tear off the part that identifies you. You can avoid identification by making a photocopy of the business-reply label, folding the photocopy, stapling it together, and dropping it in the mail. (If you don't own a copy machine, and don't want to pay the nickel or dime for a commercial copy at a print or copy shop, do it at work, thereby taking full advantage of the fringe benefits of your job.) The junk mailer legitimately may protest paying for a photocopy, but the protest will consume his precious time. Postal officials, if they receive enough of these to process, may decide that it's too much trouble to process junk mail, and ask Congress to eliminate that category. We can hope and spur this action along.

You can also voice your annoyance over junk mail by looking for a toll-free number on the mail. If there is one, dial it and politely tell the person who answers that you resent having your mail box stuffed with junk mail. Be polite; don't threaten or use obscene language. Since the company that mailed the piece will be paying for the call, their phone bill will be run up, without generating any additional business.

If you are extremely sore about junk mail, you can take a further step. If the local newspaper takes classified ads by phone, you can impersonate someone from that company to place an ad. Word the ad FREE GREEN STAMPS and include the toll-free number. Or you can spend a few dollars to have some cards printed that read FREE GREEN STAMPS or FREE SEX, or whatever you think will generate phone calls. Leave these on public bulletin boards and other spots where they'll attract attention.

The next method, although illegal, is still safe because your chances of getting caught are zilch. Go to a quick-print shop and have several thousand copies of the junk mailer's business-reply envelopes printed and drop them in the mail over several weeks. You'll cause the company untold grief as all of the empty envelopes come back, each with postage to be paid on it. Any junk mailer who tries to claim that they're forgeries will have a tough time getting the post office to believe him.

TELEPHONE SALESPERSONS

Telemarketing is the electronic equivalent of junk mail. Junk phone calls steal your time and interrupt important activities. An inopportune phone call during dinner is an intrusion, but married couples rightfully may draw the line at a sales call breaking the mood later in the evening. At other times, a harried mother may resent a telephone call that wakes up the baby. The callers themselves often have no tact or sense of delicacy.

The frequency of some calls can be annoying, with several carpet-cleaning or exterminating businesses calling week after week. When the telephone solicitors approach you directly with the nature of the call, handling them is simple. In such cases, it's usually enough to explain politely that you don't need your carpet cleaned three times a week.

Boiler Room Operators

Operators of telemarketing companies, often called boiler rooms, use more high-pressure methods. Some telemarketing solicitors will announce cheerfully (and fraudulently) that you've won a prize—a car, vacation for two, or fur coat. Others say they're conducting surveys, and that you are eligible to win a prize if you answer a few questions correctly. Some boiler-room operators may try to sell you vitamins, precious metals or some new, foolproof diet. All material offered for sale is overpriced, in order to pay for the cost of operating the boiler room and the commissions of the salesmen.

The professionals often incorporate deceptive tactics into their spiel. If they're after the lady of the house, they'll ask for her in a familiar way that suggests they're personal friends. The tip-off comes when they mispronounce the name or use an unfamiliar one.

Many consumers think the volume of telephone solicitations has reached a crisis stage in this country. In some areas, anyone who has a telephone gets a barrage of solicitations. An unlisted number rarely offers relief any more because many telephone solicitation systems dial every number sequentially. Others use a tape-recorded message and computerized dialing to hit every possible telephone number. Moreover, some companies buy lists of new numbers and even unlisted numbers from corrupt persons in the telephone company.

Law-enforcement officials have begun to crack down on illegal operations, but boiler rooms are so intensely profitable that no matter how many the police bust, new ones spring up to take their place. Operators out on bail immediately start new boiler rooms under different names. Although law-enforcement agencies are concentrating more resources against these illegal operations, people such as yourself continue to be victimized by them. What can you do to defend yourself?

Countermeasures

A polite refusal is often enough for the simple sales call. The more complex and deceptive operators call for different tactics. The quickest way is to hang up once you're sure the call is from a boiler room. Sophisticated boiler-room workers, however, are skilled at keeping you guessing, to keep you from slamming the phone down. This is why you have to screen callers.

When someone you don't recognize calls and asks for another member of the family, simply ask if they're a friend or selling something. If you're still not sure, say that person can't come to the phone and ask for a number at which the caller can be reached. The boiler-room operator will never leave a number, always saying that he or she will call back.

Don't be shy about screening callers this way. A legitimate caller won't be offended, as he or she probably gets many such nuisance calls.

A telephone-answering machine may be your most effective screening measure if you don't want to waste even a second on unwanted calls. Most answering machines allow you to listen to the message as the caller puts it on tape so you can pick up the phone if you want to speak with the caller. Legitimate callers will give their names and telephone numbers, and sometimes a short message. Boiler-room callers simply hang up.

Another effective countermeasure is to listen to the sales pitch for a minute, until you're sure it's a sales call and not a personal one. Once you're sure, you ask the person to hold on for a moment, and put down the phone. You then go on with what you were doing, and sooner or later the telephone solicitor will realize that he's been had and hang up. This method usually works because it hits them right where they live, wasting their precious time as they waste yours.

If the solicitation is one which leads to a salesperson coming by for a demonstration or delivery, you'll have an opportunity to inconvenience him even more if you're willing to spend a few minutes setting it up. The telephone solicitor will probably ask you to verify your address. If he doesn't, simply volunteer that you've recently moved and offer to give him your new address. Send the salesman to the wrong address, either to the most inconvenient spot you can imagine or—for a double payback—to the home of someone who has wronged you in some other way. If you get a callback on this, deny everything, including having spoken with the telephone solicitor or ever having lived at the address where the salesman went.

Sometimes, telephone solicitors make mistakes. They'll dial the wrong number or ask for the wrong person. This gives you another opportunity to kill two birds with one stone. Keep close at hand the name and address of someone whom you dislike, and tell the solicitor that you're that person. Send a salesman to his address. If the solicitor is selling some merchandise or service over the phone, order something expensive or embarrassing in the person's name, secure in the knowledge that it cannot be traced to you.

INSURANCE COMPANIES

Insurance companies are notorious for legalized scams that border on consumer fraud. It is no coincidence that they were the only type of business to prosper during the Great Depression. They operate profitably at all times because insurance-company managers have the system locked in to their needs. Each state has a commission to regulate insurance companies within that state, but it is staffed by insurance-company personnel to ensure that regulations suit the needs of the insurance industry. In other words, they legalize thievery. We find excellent examples of this in automobile insurance.

In states where automobile liability insurance is mandatory, rates are higher than in states where it's not. This isn't because states with mandatory insurance have higher accident rates; it's simply because insurance companies have captive clients. The most convincing evidence of this comes immediately after a mandatory-insurance law is passed, as recently happened in Arizona. Auto insurance rates immediately jumped.

One of the conditions of insurance coverage is that the premium will increase if the client has an accident that's his fault or gets a traffic citation. This is understandable, as this driver is a greater risk and will cost the carrier more than if he had a perfect driving record. However, the premium increase is always disproportional to the risk, and any policyholder who places a claim against his carrier—even if he is not at fault in any way—is likely to find his rates increased dramatically.

Moreover, some drivers with perfect records wind up with cancellations. Insurance companies brutalize consumers in states that allow cancellation of insurance without reason and with only a 30-day written notice. New York is one such state where anyone whose insurance is canceled for any reason (or even no reason) falls into what's called an assigned-risk pool, from which applicants are dealt out to companies like cards from a deck. The applicant pays a 50-percent surcharge for the same coverage he had before he was cancelled. The insurance companies, in their greed for fatter profits, realized that the accounts would come back to them anyway, but at a 50 percent increase in premiums. So they began to cancel even drivers with perfect driving records. The only recourse available to drivers who found this objectionable was to give up their cars or drive them illegally since they could not be registered without proof of insurance coverage.

What can the little guy do to fight back? A lot, if he's bold and creative.

One way to obtain a lower rate for insurance is to register your car in another locale. In some cases, you can save money by registering your car in the name of a friend or relative in an adjoining state where the rates are lower. Insurance rates will certainly be lower in a state with no mandatory-insurance requirement.

In states where insurance rates are lower for female drivers, it's worth registering both cars in a two-car family in the wife's name.

Filing claims is like walking through a minefield. Drivers often hesitate to file claims because they know that, although they'll collect, they'll pay more in higher premiums during the next few years than the claim was worth. Here's how the smart operator works the angles to his benefit.

First, he doesn't file for small claims because of the certainty of higher premiums. Instead, he waits until conditions are right, and plays it for all it's worth. An example is collision damage. If it's extensive and worth filing a claim, the driver can work out a deal with a friend or willing acquaintance in the auto-repair business to supply him with a bill for more than the actual charges, for reimbursement by the insurance company. In many cases, the insurance company will facilitate this by asking for repair estimates and issuing a check based on the estimates. It's easy to obtain written estimates from an auto repair shop known for high prices, get the check, and then take the car to a lower-priced body shop for the work. In such a case, the car owner is completely within his legal rights and earns a profit on the deal.

A car owner frequently searches for ways to collect from insurance companies when he discovers he's bought a lemon. The car is out of warranty; the dealer won't make good on it; if he tries to sell, he'll take a bath; it seems he's stuck with the lemon. Another, albeit frivolous, reason to try to collect insurance may be that the owner is simply tired of the car or of making payments on it.

The key to determining if the risk is worthwhile is

whether an insurance company pays off on a stolen or wrecked car according to depreciated or replacement value. If the policy specifies depreciated value, the client will almost always come up short because depreciation is calculated according to a formula that minimizes the company's payment, regardless of the free-market value of the car. If the insurance policy specifies replacement value, the owner has a chance of getting something worthwhile out of the insurance company.

The smart operator simply leaves the car in a bad part of town, in a neighborhood where any fairly new, unattended car will be stripped before the sun goes down. The owner files his claim, stating that the car broke down in that area; when he returned he found it stripped. Because a stripped car is usually totaled, the insurance company will pay the full value of the vehicle.

Another way to get rid of an unwanted vehicle, for those living in states bordering Mexico, is to drive the car into Mexico and sell it for cash. This will bring a fairly low price to avoid paperwork, but on returning to the States the owner reports his car stolen and collects from the insurance company also.

The final move, if there's no other way, is to set fire to the car in an isolated spot. Authorities will likely conclude that someone stole the car, took it joy-riding, and then set it afire. The insurance company will pay you the replacement value of the car.

DOCTORS
AND HOSPITALS

At times, it seems as though members of the medical profession are at war with their clients. Doctors display demeaning or even hostile attitudes toward the people whom they are supposed to be helping. Moreover, the for-profit nature of medicine in the United States leads some doctors to push unnecessary treatments on their patients.

American doctors mostly practice fee-for-service medicine. The exceptions are those working in city or county hospitals, ministering to the indigent. If you're on welfare, you're going to have to take what you get. If you're paying your own way, there's no reason to accept substandard service.

It's become a standard feature of American life that going to the doctor is hazardous to your health. First, you, the patient, are supposed to make an appointment. Usually, you show up on time, sign in, and wait. And wait. And wait. If it's your first visit, the receptionist will probably hand you a form to fill out. This form often devotes more space to your fiscal condition than your physical one. The form may ask about your social security number, employer, employer's address, credit references, and so on.

Other would-be patients fill the waiting room, all waiting to get in. When your turn comes, perhaps a half-hour after the time of the appointment, someone summons you into a small room, closes the door, and instructs you to wait some more. Finally, the doctor enters with a busy air, asks you what's wrong, and makes you feel as if you're lucky to see him at all. When it's time to pay, you may wonder what you received for your money.

Breaking the Pattern

In order to break this pattern of neglect and abuse, you must first learn not to be cowed by their intimidation tactics. Understand right from the start that doctors like to promote themselves as busy, with thriving practices. They instruct their receptionists to stack their appointments to keep their patients waiting. This suggests to the patients that they're lucky the doctor can spare them any time at all. Protect yourself by not playing their game.

The first act of defiance comes when filling out the form at the initial appointment. Answer the questions relating to your medical insurance coverage (unless you're paying cash), but ignore the other questions regarding your finances. If the receptionist asks you to complete the entire form, politely state that you're not applying for a loan, welfare, or a job. Don't be reluctant to word it exactly this way. She's not going to tell you to leave. The most she'll do is tell the doctor. If he confronts you about it, repeat what you told the receptionist. If he can't live with that, seek another doctor.

Always arrive on time for your appointment. Ask the receptionist politely if the doctor is running late. Tell her you have a busy schedule that day and you expect the doctor to be on time for the appointment.

If the doctor is running more than fifteen minutes late, get up, politely tell his receptionist that you can't afford to wait any longer, and leave. This may seem drastic, but if you let the doctor get away with it, he'll continue to walk all over you. Don't worry if the doctor complains about the way you spoke to his receptionist; this is standard intimidation tactics. If you've been polite, he has no legitimate reproach. Respond by asking him if his schedule really allows him time to see you. Point out that you are on time for your appointments, and that you expect him to keep his.

Throughout this, remain polite and cool. You have the upper hand—unless you're on welfare—because you're the one signing the check. The doctor is working for you, although many doctors try to intimidate their patients into thinking that they're doing them a favor. If the doctor doesn't suit your needs, remember that there are many more out there. Contrary to the impression they try to give their patients, the number of doctors in the United States has been increasing, to the point that many of them are hungry for work. In other words, it's a buyer's market.

Resisting Intimidation

Occasionally, doctors try to slip intimidation tactics in sideways on their patients or others. Complaining about overwork is a common tactic. A doctor may say that he puts in sixty, eighty, or even ninety hours a week taking care of his patients. The logical countermove is to reply you wouldn't want a doctor suffering from such overwork and fatigue taking care of you. The results can be surprising. The doctor may well back off and admit most of the hours were spent on call, not actually on duty.

Probably every literate person today has read the advice from consumer advisers and medical professionals to seek a second opinion before consenting to surgery or other expensive or possibly dangerous treatment. Still, we see millions of needless operations performed in this country each year, because doctors need the income to make the payments on their Mercedes, and because patients still trust their doctors far more than they should.

Recent articles have reported obstetricians/gynecologists (OB-GYNs) leaving the specialty because the cost of malpractice insurance has become too much to bear. What these specialists don't tell you is they have brought this situation upon themselves by performing unnecessary surgeries on their patients. These specialists routinely perform three of the most common operations in the United States today: hysterectomies, circumcisions, and Cesarian-section deliveries.

For several decades, the medical press has warned patients and doctors about the high rate of hysterectomies performed on American women. Various surgeons who have studied the problem have estimated that between one-third to two-thirds of hysterectomies are unnecessary. Women should always seek a second opinion and think carefully before consenting to this procedure. The OB-GYN may be the expert, but it's your body. He has many patients. You have only one body.

In recent years, the proportion of American babies delivered by Cesarian has risen to about 25 percent. It's hard to justify this medically, especially since European women still have most of their babies naturally. It's not that American doctors are any better than their European counterparts. The infant mortality rate in the United States, while dropping, is still higher than in most European countries. Medicine is big business in the United States, with a trend toward more for-profit hospitals and clinics, rather than publicly funded ones. Surgery is profitable for the doctor and the hospital, in which he typically owns stock.

Circumcision, which is elective surgery, is routinely performed on baby boys in this country without anesthesia and certainly without the babies' consent. This is in sharp contrast to Europe, where circumcision is practiced only by a few religious minorities. Doctors in this country sell circumcision to parents as a way to promote cleanliness, prevent cancer and venereal diseases, and make him look like his father and schoolmates. Lately, some doctors have claimed it may help prevent AIDS. AIDS rates in Europe are far lower than in the United States, and their male population doesn't seem to suffer any huge public-health problems as a result of growing up uncircumcised.

Doctors also assure new parents that circumcision is a risk-free procedure, scarcely more significant than clipping toenails. Of course, this isn't quite accurate. The 8 October 1985 issue of *The New York Times* reported the story of two boys circumcised on the same day in an Atlanta hospital who both lost their penises from burns caused by electrocautery. Not surprisingly, both incidents resulted in lawsuits, according to the article.

With such profuse and reckless surgery, it's no wonder OB-GYNs encounter more than what they believe is their share of lawsuits—despite the difficulty of finding a doctor to testify against another.

The lesson for you is clear. Avoid surgery if at all possible. The doctor may be seeking to make the next payment on his Mercedes with your blood. The term "remunerectomy" was coined specifically to describe these fee-inspired operations.

Hospitals

If you've seen a hospital bill recently, you understand why Americans are spending so much on health care and getting so little. Not only are room charges astronomical, but hospitals also charge inflated prices for every item used by a patient. An aspirin costs a dollar or two. A box of tissues or a bottle of hydrogen peroxide goes at jacked-up prices. Such practices are a primary reason outpatient surgical facilities have become so popular. Although outpatient units don't provide discount rates, they charge much less because they have the patient within their walls for only a few hours.

If you're unfortunate enough to need hospitalization, you'll find that the exorbitant prices you pay buy only shoddy and uncaring services. The basic fact is: hospital staffs run hospitals for their convenience, not the patient's. Only in emergency rooms can you expect immediate and responsive treatment. Elsewhere, you'll be lucky if the nurse brings your medicine on schedule. The quality of the food in some hospitals, which rivals in price that of some of the finest restaurants, is worse than on airlines, usually cold, unhealthy, and unappetizing.

Another pernicious practice in some of today's hospitals is heavy drugging of patients. Drugged patients don't make demands or complaints, and doctors and nurses work together to keep their charges quiet so their jobs are easier. A doped-up patient is less likely to notice cold food or late medicine. Even if he does, he's less likely to complain forcefully to hospital staff.

The point is obvious: stay out of hospitals if you can. Once admitted, you're on their ground and have to play by their rules. If hospitalization is absolutely unavoidable, you (not the doctor) should choose the hospital. Rely on word-of-mouth reports from friends and relatives and published reviews of hospital ratings, not the doctor's judgment. This may mean changing doctors, but it's worth it because your doctor will only admit you to hospitals in which he enjoys a cozy working relationship. This usually means that he has a piece of the action.

Once admitted, have a trusted friend or relative visit you each day to monitor your treatment. As a patient, your complaints about maltreatment will be almost meaningless unless you document them. If, for example, the nurse wakes you during the night to take a sleeping pill, make a written note of it and tell your friend during the next visit. If your nurse brings your medicine late or not at all, document that, too. Your friend or relative should voice the complaint because he'll be able to get and retain the hospital staff's attention better than you. Nurses are experts at dismissing patients' complaints and making excuses for themselves if the doctor should inquire.

If something goes seriously wrong, document that, too. Postoperative bleeding, for example, can be quite serious. If your nurses ignore it, or even if they seem to respond, tell your visitors about the bleeding. This can make a lot of difference if you later decide to sue.

The time to prepare for a lawsuit is before making the decision. Keeping a written record of when you requested services and when they were delivered will better support you courtroom testimony than your unsupported memory. If possible, have a friend photocopy your hospital chart if he can reach it without risking discovery. A report of postoperative bleeding, for example, can substantiate a claim you may later make in court. The absence of a notation on your chart (if you can prove through the eyewitness testimony of your visitors that you reported the bleeding to hospital staff) indicates sloppy record keeping and can go a long way towards proving malpractice.

More important than proving malpractice is saving your life. If you become convinced that your doctor or the hospital is not taking proper care of you, get out! If you can, walk. If you cannot, have a friend or relative aid you. As long as you're confined to the hospital, you're under the control of its staff.

Leave immediately and find another doctor. Both the doctor and hospital will try to stop you from seeking help elsewhere. They will throw a legal term at you: leaving against medical advice. They are trying to intimidate you into remaining in their hands. Once convinced of your intention to leave, hospital personnel will try to force you to sign a release form before you leave. Remember that you don't have to sign *anything*. Before being admitted, you must sign various permission forms and releases from liability or they won't admit you. However, when leaving (even against medical advice), they can't force you to sign anything. If they try to keep you there, get a witness and ask to see the administrator. When he arrives, inform him that your attorney will be very interested in the hospital's attempts to retain you against your will.

For emphasis, remember not to sign anything when you leave against their wishes. They can't make you sign release or discharge forms or anything else. Pay your bill and go. Signing would weaken your case if it goes to court.

Self-Defense against the Medical Establishment

It's unfortunate that hospitals, doctors, and nurses have become your adversaries rather than your benefactors. Their main motivation seems to be to obtain as much money as they can from you while doing as little as possible to earn it. In dealing with them, you must be wary. Not only is your money on the line, but you're entrusting your body to people who care very little about your welfare. Frankly, the only one who will look out for you is yourself.

PARKING CITATIONS

Most cities have too few parking spaces for the number of cars who need (or want) them, so competition is fierce. If you must park in the center of town regularly, you'll find hordes of meter maids and police officers waiting to pounce on your car the moment you walk away, just waiting for the flag to pop up.

One way to avoid a ticket is to leave the hood up, as if you have had a breakdown. This may fool some police officers. Another common trick is to put an old parking ticket under your windshield wiper before you walk away. (This ploy may fool a young police officer just out of the academy, but don't count on it working with experienced patrol officers.)

PROTECTING
YOUR ASSETS

Protecting your assets can be difficult in many situations, unless you're in the top-income bracket, which allows you to hire a staff of asset-protection specialists who will ensure that you retain what's yours. Most of us can't afford top-flight attorneys and certified public accountants to look after our finances.

If you're down among the rest of us, you can be extremely vulnerable in certain situations, but perhaps none quite so much as during a divorce. Your spouse, with the advice of a good attorney, can milk your assets mercilessly.

Personal liability also threatens your financial security. Today, you can be sued for almost anything. Lawsuits have become big business in this country, and personal-injury attorneys are flourishing as a result. For most people, being sued is like being struck by lightning. "Why me?" they ask. Well, why not you? Somebody has to be the victim.

Divorce

Divorce is rarely neat and sweet. Deterioration of a relationship usually results in a backlog of hate and bitterness, and it's hard for the parties to deal with the issues rationally and logically. In many cases the woman, who usually has the upper hand, will tell her spouse outright, "I'm going to make you pay, sucker!" Women often can gain sympathy from friends, neighbors, judges, and police officers by simply breaking into tears. Additionally, they can claim wife abuse, which doesn't necessarily involve a brutal beating. This often puts the husband at a disadvantage, even if he never laid a hand on her. A good liar can explain her way around the lack of scars and bruises by claiming that the husband threatened to beat her or slapped her in places that don't show bruises. If the husband has a reputation for a short temper or was ever foolish enough to make verbal threats in front of others, he's lost the case before it starts.

Divorce settlements seem to be most unpleasant when children are involved. Some women may even claim that the father has abused the children. In today's climate, an accusation, particularly of sexual abuse, is almost the same as a conviction because in many instances no definite physical symptoms are necessary. Some wives have used this tactic successfully to harass their husbands and win custody of the children.

Self-Protection in a Divorce

The person who files for divorce has the initiative and the advantage of being able to plan his actions. Self-protection starts long before filing the papers in court. Once the legal battle starts, it's too late to do anything except react. Self-protection for a divorce involves seizing the initiative and never letting go, thereby keeping the other party on the defensive.

One of the first actions in a contested divorce is to get control of the cash. Whoever moves first grabs the bank account and leaves the other party nothing with which to pay day-to-day expenses. In one sense, this tactic victimizes the husband less because he usually has a job. With his next paycheck, he can start replenishing his cash supply, and if he has a couple of credit cards for cushioning, he can soon get back on his feet.

Although credit cards have their uses, particularly during the uncertainties of divorce, they also can be serious liabilities. A spiteful wife may go on one last spending spree knowing her husband is usually liable for her expenditures, especially if she doesn't work. Before telling her about the divorce action, the husband should simply take the wife's cards out of her purse and destroy them if possible. If this proves difficult, he should close out the accounts before starting the divorce action.

The divorce settlement will divide assets between the husband and wife. Commonly, one party will try to conceal assets during the proceedings. This only works if the wife truly knows little or nothing about her husband's business or finances, and if her attorney and the judge aren't looking out for her welfare. In any case, both parties usually have to sign statements that the assets they declare are all they possess, and that any others subsequently uncovered will become part of the settlement.

If you wish to hide assets, you must begin long before a divorce seems possible. You should never allow your wife to know all of your business, and you should always keep an ace in the hole about which your wife knows nothing. Close scrutiny of financial transactions focuses around the time of the divorce, not those taking place a decade before. As you can see, this is part of keeping a low profile, a fundamental principle that applies in all aspects of your life.

It's illegal to withhold financial records from your

spouse if there is a court order, but if there isn't one, why give these valuable records to her attorney to use against you until you have to?

"Possession is nine-tenths of the law" may be a cliché, but it applies strongly during a divorce. Let's consider the hypothetical case of a couple with no children, living in a rented apartment. One day the husband comes home from work to find a bare apartment. His wife has removed the furniture while he was at work. She left no forwarding address. The husband knows that he could sue to recover his half of the furniture, but being practical, what's he going to do that night? How much will it cost to sue? How long will it take to recover what's legitimately his? Effectively, she's gotten away with grand theft.

Another frequent occurrence is that of the husband who is met by changed locks and a police officer with a court order when he comes home. The husband is then required to take his personal belongings and leave his wife in possession of their home.

These two instances illustrate the importance of preempting the other party. If the husband believes that the marriage is beyond repair, he should make the first move before the wife is even aware of his decision. He should consider carefully other tactics as well, including moving to another state with more favorable divorce laws.

Moving out of state can solve several problems. The wife may have to file for divorce in the state of his residency. If he takes the children, it often puts them out of her reach. Moving to another country is even more effective, especially if the wife has filed kidnapping charges against him for taking the children. Certain Latin American countries, such as Argentina, have laws favoring the husband in divorce and child-custody cases.

Liability

Getting sued is both unpleasant and hazardous to your financial health. In this section we'll discuss it from two viewpoints. The first is preventing or forestalling a lawsuit; the second, protecting what you have in anticipation of getting sued. Note the cautious phrasing: in anticipation of getting sued. Prevention is better than cure.

Prevention means avoiding things that can get you sued. Some situations, such as traffic accidents, are almost unavoidable, but others are easily avoidable. Avoiding a high-risk occupation is one protective measure. As we've already seen, obstetricians and gynecologists face excessive lawsuits and malpractice insurance premiums, resulting in part from the unnecessary surgeries and other abusive treatments which have occurred in that specialty. To avoid liability suits and exorbitant malpractice insurance, many OB-GYNs have quit the specialty to practice general medicine. So have other medical specialists with unusually high lawsuits and insurance coverage, including neurosurgeons and anesthesiologists. However, all doctors are targets for lawsuits because most are affluent or are perceived to be by the public.

Keeping a Low Profile

Occasionally, we read of a hermit dying and leaving a vast amount of money in his mattress. He kept a low profile. Nobody would think of suing anyone who dressed shabbily and lived in the poor part of town. Keeping a low profile means keeping your real wealth secret. It involves living modestly and letting nobody know your real worth.

Maintaining a low profile also means not driving an expensive car, not having custom license plates, not wearing expensive jewelry or clothing, and not taking expensive trips, as far as your friends and neighbors know. If you must fly to Europe on the Concorde, don't tell your friends and neighbors about it. Buy tickets to Newark, New Jersey, instead and tell your friends that you're going to visit relatives in Hoboken. Take a helicopter to Kennedy Airport and catch the Concorde there. Also, don't install an expensive swimming pool, buy a giant-screen TV, or show any other signs of obvious wealth.

What do you do with your assets to both protect them and maintain a low profile? No completely satisfactory answer exists. Keeping your assets in a bank account in the United States is not the answer because banks report the interest earnings to the Internal Revenue Service and, with a court order, will release financial information to your spouse's attorney or to the court. Keeping an account in an assumed name can be done, but withdrawing funds can be difficult. Banks often ask for more identification for withdrawals than they do for deposits.

Some people think that investments are harder to trace, but stocks and bonds leave paper trails, just as do bank accounts. Also, unless you're a stockbroker, you have to buy and sell stocks and bonds through a broker, who collects a commission on each transaction.

Putting your money into compact valuables has its advantages. Diamonds, precious metals, or stamps leave less of a paper trail for someone to trace. They also can be bought under an assumed name, and they're easy to store inconspicuously. Don't use a safe deposit box in a bank, however, because banks report their transactions to tax authorities. A better choice is a private vault, and consumers usually have several companies to choose from since their number is multiplying for just this reason. Some people choose to hide or bury valuables for later excavation.

One problem with compact valuables is that they cannot always be readily redeemed for cash. In most instances, unless you find a private buyer, you have to work through a dealer, and he gets his cut. This amounts to paying a tax on the transaction, just as with stocks and bonds. The best reason for stockpiling light and transportable valuables is as a reserve for fleeing the country.

One safe way to create hidden assets requires a partner who is a businessman. If you are a silent partner in a business, you have a potentially secret asset that can also be an income source. The obvious problem with this approach is that of trust: the more secret and untraceable your holdings, the more you have to trust your partner. Security in business dealings comes from putting the relationships down on paper in the form of contracts. Making these official and binding requires notarizing them or filing them with a local, county, or state office. This makes them traceable. It protects you from a dishonest partner but leaves you vulnerable during a divorce or lawsuit.

Liability Insurance

What you need to know about liability insurance is simple: if the coverage is adequate, the policy isn't affordable. Many small property owners (house, car, and personal possessions) have liability-insurance policies that cover the total value of what they own, presumably to provide an umbrella. Unfortunately, most people's total worth is considerably less than $100,000, and lawsuits can easily be for millions. Granted, the amount often gets whittled down in court, but you can still lose everything.

If your property adds up to $100,000 and your insurance policy is for the same amount, what do you do against a judgment of $250,000? The court will strip you of everything you have and order you to make time payments to the plaintiff for the balance left unpaid by the insurance.

Transfer of Assets

Most people don't try to transfer assets until it's too late. Consider the doctor who gets hit with a whopping malpractice suit. Afraid of losing, he transfers all he owns to his wife, who then divorces him. Doctors sometimes try this silly ploy because they genuinely believe they're so much smarter than everyone else and that the plaintiff, his attorney, and the judge will be fooled by this tactic.

The time to transfer assets is long before any suit looms on the horizon. The reason is that the plaintiff and his attorney will be going over your finances with a fine-tooth comb, but only from about the time of the incident that provoked the lawsuit. If you set up a trust fund for a child five years before the incident, that money is generally untouchable.

THE FINAL CHOICES

Most of time when we owe money, we're obligated to pay it back. Banks, credit companies, and the government will join forces to squeeze it out of us, especially if we owe back taxes. However, just as it's true that you can't get blood out of a stone, you also can't get money out of a corpse. This gives the person unfortunate enough to have a terminal illness a powerful advantage.

Anyone who knows he has only a few months to live faces the problem of what to do with the rest of his life, short as it will be. He can't make any long-range plans, but he can choose to live the high life for as long as he can. He does this by using credit, knowing that he'll never have to repay it.

First, you should stop paying on any current debts. What's the point in making any more payments on a house or car if you won't live long enough to enjoy them? The same goes for taxes. Save your cash for immediate needs.

If you have a good credit record, your chances are better

than fifty-fifty of stalling creditors and government alike until it's too late for them to collect from you. To ensure success, don't reveal your terminal illness. This makes you more of a credit risk, compromising your chances of extending your credit limits.

It's not just creditors from whom you should withhold news of your illness. You should tell as few people as possible because some creditors send out investigators who might extract the information from your friends and associates. If you have to stop working, think up a reason to give your employer, but don't mention your affliction.

Buying time becomes your main objective. Learn all the ways to hold off creditors for a few days or weeks without arousing suspicion. You can forget to put a check in the envelope with the invoice. Or send the telephone company a check made out to the electric company and vice versa. Having insufficient funds in your account will result in the check being returned and a charge against your account, but it will buy you time. Another common trick is to forget to sign your checks.

The examples above are simple stalling techniques. At this point you may decide that you want to play games with your creditors' minds. This involves more complex methods. One is to note on your check that this is payment in full, but make the check out for less than the amount owed. If the creditor deposits the check, this may get you off the hook. If he catches the discrepancy, he'll return your check, perhaps with a letter from his attorney.

Another ruse would be to notify your bank that your checkbook has been stolen and request a stop payment on all checks outstanding. Getting a letter from the bank to substantiate this will help you hold off your creditors for a while, presumably while you set up another account and write checks from it.

You might try outright forgery to settle a debt. Write a check for only a small part of what you owe. This will certainly provoke a demand for payment in full. When you get the check back with your statement, write out another for the total amount and photocopy the face of that check. Also photocopy the back of the check that cleared, and send them both to your creditor with a letter stating that you paid in full, and here are the photocopies to prove it.

These paper games will confuse and delay your creditors for a while, but they'll catch up with you eventually. If you try any of these with the expectation of a long life, this will give your creditors time to take action. They are designed to be used only when you have very little time left.

If you need to stall a creditor on a larger debt, claim a grievance. If it's a car, bring it in to the dealer and ask that he correct a nonexistent noise in the engine or transmission. Then write to the bank and advise them that the car is defective and that you're not going to make any more payments until the dealer provides satisfaction. Months can go by before they sort out the problem.

In the meantime, you may get a few phone calls regarding the delinquent payment. Although federal law now prohibits some of the more deceptive and unfair debt-collection tactics, you can still expect to be dunned. Some collectors call late at night to catch you when you're most likely to be home.

To avoid these collectors, never answer the telephone directly. To be sure, pull the plug on your phone so that it doesn't ring at all. Buy a telephone answering machine, if you don't already have one, and use it twenty-four hours a day, screening calls even when you are home.

Another area you might consider is applying for more

credit. This usually isn't hard at all, because almost anyone with a good credit record is bombarded with junk mail advertising credit cards from banks and finance companies around the country. Fill out as many as you can, exaggerating your income. The worst they can do is turn down your application.

Having several checking accounts allows you to stretch your money for a while. Open accounts at as many banks as possible and put as little cash as possible in each account. Checking accounts aren't as valuable as credit cards for the traveler, but merchants usually accept checks from local residents who have two pieces of identification. You can buy several thousand dollars' worth of merchandise using checks from various accounts, each one holding only a couple hundred dollars.

Finally, liquidate all assets. This means either converting everything to cash or giving it away to family and friends. This is to avoid leaving anything that either the government or the credit companies can seize to recover the debts.

You should concentrate on spending the line of credit of each card. To do this, you must know the predetermined limit of each card. If you attempt to go beyond this ceiling, the transactions won't be approved. Merchants will accept credit cards without calling in for approval when the amount is below a certain figure set by the credit-card issuer, usually fifty or one-hundred dollars. You should know it for each credit card you have.

Sooner or later you'll wear out a particular card by overspending. To get the most from each card and to extend its period of usefulness, you should use them in sequence, saving some available credit for later use. The most efficient way to extend a credit card is to make big purchases first, such as airline tickets. Businesses contact the credit-card issuer to obtain authorization only for the large amounts. Once you've exceeded the limit on a card, you can use it only for amounts too small to call in for authorization.

One smart way of maximizing a credit card's usefulness is by using it for items you can convert easily to cash later, such as airline tickets. Once the paperwork is in your hands, you can cash it in at any airport in the country. (This trick works even better with checks, because you can buy several sets of airline tickets with checks from the same account. It'll be several days before the checks bounce, which allows you time enough to cash in the tickets.) If you buy your tickets at a travel agency that sells traveler's checks, you can buy a supply of these, too. Once they're in your hands, they're as good as cash anywhere in the world.

After you've worn out a credit card, discard it and switch to a fresh one from a different bank. In setting up your sequence, you should use the credit card and checks from the same bank at the same time. Otherwise, you'll probably find a hold on your credit card from a bank at which you've overdrawn your checking account.

Of course, all these transactions are fraudulent and easily prosecuted because you have documented each step of the way. However, if you're in the last days of your life, you have little to lose. No court can (or would) impose a meaningful sentence on you. Even if fraud brought capital punishment (which it doesn't in any state in the United States), all that might do is bring to an end the painful, final stage of a fatal illness.

AFTERWORD

No, Virginia, there is no Santa Claus. However, if you play your cards right, you may not need one. Be your own Santa Claus.